NOW YOU CAN READ....
MOSES in the BULRUSHES

STORY RETOLD BY ELAINE IFE

ILLUSTRATED BY ERIC ROWE

Published by Rourke Publications, Inc. P.O. Box 868,
Windermere, Florida 32786. Copyright © 1983 by Rourke
Publications, Inc. All copyrights reserved. No part of this
book may be reproduced in any form without written per-
mission from the publisher. Printed in the United States of
America.
 The Publishers acknowledge permission from Brimax
Books for the use of the name "Now You Can Read" and
"Large Type For First Readers" which identify Brimax Now
You Can Read series.

Library of Congress Cataloging in Publication Data

Ife, Elaine, 1955-
 Moses in the bulrushes.

 (Now you can read—Bible stories)
 Summary: Recounts the incident in which the baby
Moses was saved from certain death by the king of Egypt's
daughter.
 1. Moses (Biblical leader)—Juvenile literature.
[1. Moses (Biblical leader) 2. Bible stories—O.T.]
I. Rowe, Eric, 1938- ill. II. Title. III. Series.
BS580.M6I37 1983   222'.1209505   83-13812
ISBN 0-86625-217-7

GROLIER ENTERPRISES CORP.

NOW YOU CAN READ....

MOSES in the BULRUSHES

Long ago, in a country called Egypt, there lived a girl named Miriam. She was twelve years old. Her hair was long and dark, and her face was gentle. She had a brother called Aaron. He was a good boy and helped his father with the work. Their mother had another child, a little boy. He was a happy baby. He laughed and smiled at them from his cradle.

They all lived in a small, dark
house, near a great river called
the Nile. It was warm during the
day but cold at night in that
little house.

Not far away stood a great white palace. It was where the king lived. He was the ruler of Egypt and he was a proud and cruel man. He wanted to be king of Egypt for as long as he lived. He did not want anyone else to take his place.

Miriam came from a good family and her friends were good people, but the king did not like them. He had a very cruel plan. He said that every baby boy had to be killed.

Outside the big white palace marched the soldiers who guarded the king. They were hard and cruel like the king.

When they heard what the king wanted, they said they would help him. They would go to the houses and take away every baby boy. They would throw them into the river.

Miriam said, "What shall we do, mother? I do not want the soldiers to find my little brother and take him away."

"Do not be afraid, Miriam," said her mother. "I have a plan, wait and see."

As the baby was three months old, he was a strong child and his crying was very loud. His mother was worried that one of the king's cruel soldiers would hear him.

She picked some bulrushes from behind the house.

She made a basket, shaped like a cradle. On the outside, she spread black tar, so that the water could not get in. Inside, she put a lovely soft cloth.

Then, very gently, she put the baby into the basket and called to Miriam. "Come with me and be very quiet. I want you to help me and do what I say."

They crept down to the side of the river and looked for a good place to put the basket. It could not go where the water ran or it would float away.

They hid the basket in a clump of bulrushes and Miriam sat down behind it.

"You must stay here, Miriam," said
her mother. "Watch the basket.
This is just the place where the
king's daughter comes to swim. She
will find your little brother here.
She will take him to the palace.
If she does, then he will be safe."

Miriam sat very still behind the
bulrushes. She was afraid.
Before long, she
heard voices and
girls laughing.
The princess was
walking along the
path. A slave
held a sunshade
over her.

Miriam held her breath. Her little brother had begun to cry, for he was hungry by that time.

"What's that?" called the princess. "A basket is hidden there. Go and bring it to me."

One of the
servant girls
paddled out
into the
water.

She lifted up
the basket and
took it back to
the princess.
She lifted the
lid. There was
the poor baby,
crying and
kicking his
legs.

The princess didn't know much about babies, but she picked him up and cuddled him. Soon he was quiet.

"What a lovely child!" she cried.
"I would like to keep him."

Miriam stood up
and walked
forward.
"Do you need a
nurse for your
baby? I know
someone who
would be pleased
to help you," she
said.
"Yes," said the
princess. "I do
need a nurse.
Will you bring
her to me?"

Miriam ran home and told her mother what had happened. They hurried back to where the princess was waiting.

"You may take him away and look after him," said the princess to Miriam's mother. "I shall see that you are paid. When he is older you must bring him back to me."

So Miriam, the baby and their mother went back to the dark, little house. They lived there safely. When the baby was older, his mother took him to the palace. The princess loved the little boy and she called him Moses.

All these appear in the pages of the story. Can you find them?

mother

Miriam

king

baby

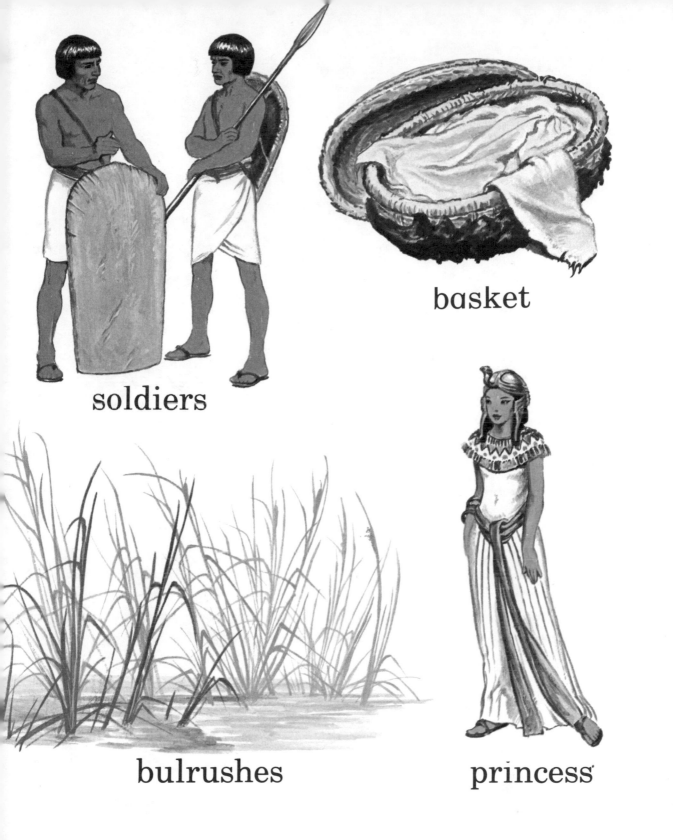

soldiers

basket

bulrushes

princess

Now tell the story in your own words.